Understanding

the

Covenant

of

Partnership

Study Guide

KENNETH COPELAND

KCM

Understanding
the
Covenant
of
Partnership

Study Guide

KENNETH COPELAND

KENNETH

COPELAND

PUBLICATIONS

Unless otherwise noted, all scripture is from the *King James Version* of the Bible.

Scripture quotations marked *The Amplified Bible* are from *The Amplified Bible, Old Testament* © 1965, 1987 by The Zondervan Corporation. *The Amplified New Testament* © 1958, 1987 by The Lockman Foundation. Used by permission.

Understanding the Covenant of Partnership Study Guide

ISBN 1-57562-695-0   30-0731

07 06 05 04 03   6 5 4 3 2

© 2002 Eagle Mountain International Church, Incorporated, aka Kenneth Copeland Publications

Kenneth Copeland Publications
Fort Worth, Texas 76192-0001

For more information about Kenneth Copeland Ministries, call 1-800-600-7395 or visit www.kcm.org.

Introduction

Gloria and I are thrilled that you have become Partners with us in ministry!

We also consider it an honor to be part of your becoming all that God has created you to be—a victorious, world overcomer. Our partnership in helping you increase in that victory is a responsibility we take seriously.

In fact, if you've known Gloria and me for any length of time, you've probably figured out by now that we go everywhere we go, say everything we say and do everything we do—all for our Partners. Our Partners mean the world to us, each and every one of them.

In 1967, Gloria and I became partners in ministry with Dr. Oral Roberts. We committed to help support his ministry through prayer and finances. As soon as we stepped out in faith and made that commitment, we immediately began to notice an increase of faith, provision and power in our lives. It was something that far exceeded what we could have ever come up with ourselves.

What happened?

We had literally tapped into the supernatural flow of anointings in Dr. Robert's life and ministry.

You see, in God's plan, partnership is all about the *anointing*. It's about getting the burden-removing, yoke-destroying power of God equally distributed among all His people.

The Bible calls us the Body of Christ. The Greek word *Christ* literally translates as "the Anointed One and His Anointing."

Certainly, *Christ* refers to Jesus. He alone was the promised Christ, the Messiah, the Holy One sent by God. But after Jesus left this earth and returned to heaven, He was able to impart that anointing through the Holy Spirit whom the Father sent to us (John 14:16 and 16:7).

That's why we are called the Body of *Christ*. We are *Christ*-ians—

anointed ones. We are the Body of God's anointing in the earth, today.

Ephesians 4:16 says, "From whom the whole body fitly joined together and compacted by that which every joint supplieth, according to the effectual working in the measure of every part...."

That simply means no one person—not even the apostle, the prophet, the evangelist, the pastor or the teacher—has it all. No one man or woman of God has the complete manifested Anointing of God. But together—we do.

Each one of us has a God-given supply of anointing to offer the rest of the Body. You have a supply of God's anointing that I need. I have a supply of God's anointing that you need, and so on. But in order for that anointing to flow among us in its greatest potential, we must join together. We must become divinely connected.

How?

Through *partnership.*

God's Word tells us that partnership in ministry is the most powerful relationship on the face of this earth. It is a covenant relationship based on the blood of Jesus. It is a relationship of the highest honor. Consequently, it is a relationship of the highest commitment.

It is because of this high level of commitment that I want you to fully understand all the aspects of being a Covenant Partner with Kenneth Copeland Ministries. It is important for you to know exactly what you are committing to as you come into this relationship. It is just as important for you to have an idea of what to expect from us.

With that in mind, I have set down in "black and white" for you the fundamental principles of partnership that the Spirit of God has taught me in my own life and ministry in the past 36 years. These principles are the very heartbeat of this ministry. They are who we are. But they also speak of the place where I believe the entire Body of Christ is headed very soon.

I am convinced that these principles of partnership are the keys to our victory in the last days. They are the keys to supernatural increase and maximum effectiveness in the end-time harvest. They are the keys to the coming together of the Body of Christ in unity and full manifestation of the ministry gifts.

Once believers begin walking in the resources and power available through partnership in ministry, the Church will absolutely explode with power. What's more, as we connect through partnership to all the anointings God has deposited in and on ministries and churches, we will become fully supplied...lacking nothing.

If it's stronger faith you're needing these days, more anointing or an increase in a particular area of your life, study the principles contained in the pages that follow. Don't just read the material lightly and take my word that it's true. Get out your Bible and note pad and dig in. Allow the Holy Spirit to reveal it to you personally.

That's why we set this book up to be more of a Bible study for you to *work* through. Take the time necessary to go through the scriptures in each chapter, meditate on them and allow God's Spirit to give you fresh revelation.

I guarantee that if you will believe and act on these principles of partnership, you will tap into a spiritual gold mine—one so deep and so rich, you will never be able to plumb the depths of it in this lifetime.

You've already made the commitment to join us in partnership. Now, learn how you can spiritually share the full scope of God's anointing and materially receive exceeding abundantly above all that you ask or think.

Yes, *partnership* is about commitment. But it's also about an unlimited supply of Holy Ghost power.

That's why Gloria and I are committed to you. That's why we carry you in our hearts everywhere we go. *Together,* we are going to change this world through the power of partnership.

Kenneth Copeland

1

"...The whole body fitly joined together and compacted by that which every joint supplieth, according to the effectual working in the measure of every part, maketh increase of the body unto the edifying of itself in love."

Ephesians 4:16

CHAPTER ONE
The Power and Purpose
of Partnership

God Designed Partnership as a Means of Manifesting His Anointing in the Earth

The Power of God Through the Power of Partnership

I once read the story of an interesting and powerful man named Benjamin O. Davis Jr.

Gen. Davis was the first African American to graduate from the U.S. Military Academy in the 20th century. During World War II, he led the Tuskegee Airmen into combat, forming the most successful fighter pilot wing in U.S. history. He later became America's first black Air Force general, and was instrumental in the U.S. armed forces becoming integrated.

But amid all those crowning achievements, there was something about this man that caught my attention.

Davis had gone through four years as a cadet at West Point without ever making a friend. His reason was simply, "No one ever approached me to be my friend." Davis felt as though all the other cadets merely tolerated him—and only because they had to. He described those years as the loneliest of his life.

As I read this, I could almost hear the countless voices of people in the Church today saying the same thing.

"Sure, I go to church, Brother Copeland, but I really don't feel at home there. I don't feel accepted. I don't feel connected."

With churches overflowing with people who don't "feel connected," it's no wonder that Christians have been gathering together for the past 1,000 years, begging God for something they already had—power. Power to do miracles, to work signs and wonders and to help save a lost and dying world.

Indeed, for centuries the Church has had access to that power but it has been divided, disconnected, and consequently, powerless.

We have not seen the power of God manifesting in the Church the way it should have because we have not known the power of *partnership*. We never made the connection between God's power and our partnership. ༺༝

Dare to Cross the Line

In the case of Gen. Davis, it's interesting that no one was more surprised to hear his commentary on his days at West Point than his classmates.

Their observation of this promising cadet was that Davis showed every potential of becoming an outstanding leader. Oddly enough, however, to them he never seemed interested in having anything to do with anyone.

There was no question that Cadet Davis was smart, studious and very determined to fulfill the vision he had for his life, even against all the opposition he faced. But all the potential and determination in the world could not offset the fact that he had isolated himself those four years.

> *We come together for the sake of Jesus— for His cause and for what He has called us to do.*

Here was a class of white cadets with one black cadet, divided by race. Sadly, neither side knew how to connect with one another. At best, they co-existed. They certainly never connected.

Each one of those young men—as well as the American people as a whole—could have benefited much earlier on— and to a much greater degree—had they known anything about God's ways of doing things.

As it turned out, Davis and the other officers of his class did come together and were some of the most powerful men of the 20th century. But it took a war to begin to bring them together.

Today, it's no different with the Church.

As the Body of Christ, we need to understand that we don't *have church* just so we can have a place to hang out, or so we can be around people who treat us with a little respect.

No, we come together as the Church for the sake of Jesus—for the sake of His cause and for what He has called us to do.

The Apostle Paul wrote to the Church at Philippi and said: "I thank my God upon every remembrance of you, always in every prayer of mine for you...for your *fellowship in the gospel...*" (Philippians 1:3-5).

Here, the word *fellowship* can also be translated as "partnership." It describes a covenant relationship between two parties who have common interests. The purpose of their partnership, or covenant relationship, is to accomplish something that neither of them could do alone.

When we take this definition a step further, we find that the literal meaning of the Greek word translated as *fellowship* is "communion," which gives even more emphasis to partnership being a matter of covenant.

In reality, Paul was telling his covenant partners in Philippi, "I thank God for your *communion* with me in this gospel." Paul knew he could not minister the gospel alone—and neither could the Philippians. It took all of them, together. That was Jesus' cause. That was God's plan.

The Advantages in Life

God designed partnership to give us—the Body of His anointed ones—the advantage over everything else in this world, and over everyone else. We don't have *an* advantage. We have *the* advantage.

For the most part, though, people in the Church are unaware of this God-given advantage. Over a period of time the Church did not teach about the anointing. Religious leaders started saying that God's anointing had passed away and was no longer in operation.

Well, of course, it wasn't in operation. Christians stopped exercising their faith and choosing to walk in it. So it just sat there untapped and unused.

We are carriers of Almighty God's burden-removing, yoke-destroying power.

Again, it was Paul who said, "Unto every one of us is given grace according to the measure of the gift of Christ" (Ephesians 4:7).

Grace according to the measure of the gift of Christ...sounds great. But what did Paul mean by it?

To begin with, it helps to know that the word translated as *grace* in this passage refers to the "anointing" of God. Actually, *grace* and *anointing* can be used interchangeably.

We also need to know that *Christ* is a Greek word that can be translated as "the Anointed One," referring directly to Jesus, the Anointed Son of God. It can also be translated as "anointing" when referring directly to power with which God anointed Jesus.

So, when Paul used the word *Christ* in Ephesians 4:7, he was referring to the anointing; therefore, we can translate this verse as follows: "Unto every one of us is given [anointing] according to the measure of the gift of [the anointing]."

Paul understood that the actual, physical body of Jesus was the residing place of God's anointing while He lived and ministered on this earth in the flesh. Then, when Jesus ascended into heaven, that full embodiment of anointing went with Him.

But then God did something no one expected. He sent His Spirit back into the earth, back into men. And that's what Paul was referring to in this verse.

Today, you and I are that Body of Jesus. We are that Body of God's anointing in the earth. We are carriers of Almighty God's burden-removing, yoke-destroying power (Isaiah 10). While none of us alone contains the full measure of that power, together we do—which is where *partnership* comes into play.

In Ephesians 4, Paul went on to say that when Jesus ascended into heaven, He gave gifts unto men (verse 8). Paul listed those gifts in verses 11-12: "And [Jesus] gave some, apostles; and some, prophets; and some, evangelists; and some, pastors and teachers; for the perfecting of the saints, for the work of the ministry, for the edifying of the body of Christ [the Anointed One and His Anointing]."

When God calls ministers of the gospel, He anoints them and gives them as gifts to the Body. That does not make them more special than anyone else. They are members of the Body of anointed ones like the rest of us.

But once God sends these "gifts"—the apostles, prophets, evangelists, pastors and teachers—and sets them among us, it is His Anointing on them which begins to perfect us through revelation.

Over time, then, God begins to move among us, prompting us to connect with these "gifts" through partnership, bringing us into covenant relationship with them. Once that divine connection is made, the anointing that is on the apostle, prophet, evangelist, pastor or teacher is released to us. We partake of their grace, or their anointing.

Remember how Paul wrote to his covenant partners in Philippi concerning their *"fellowship* in the gospel" (Philippians 1:5)?

Well, he went on to tell them, "...Ye all are partakers of my grace [my anointing]" (verse 7).

In other words, the same anointings and giftings that were in full manifestation in Paul's life and ministry were available to those who were in covenant partnership with him. All they had to do was lay hold of it by faith, place a draw on it and receive it.

You're in the Driver's Seat

In 1967, I enrolled as a student at Oral Roberts University and was immediately hired as co-pilot for Dr. Roberts' flight crew. Not long afterward I was asked to be Dr. Roberts' driver when he traveled out of town. I would fly him wherever he went, then drive him to and from the hotels and meetings.

It was during those days that I had the privilege of being close by as Dr. Roberts preached and ministered to the people. From that vantage point, I noticed the care and attention Dr. Roberts gave to his covenant partners everywhere he went. He had the same love and respect for them as the Apostle Paul had for his partners.

It was also in that time that I decided Gloria and I needed to become partners with Dr. Roberts. I remember committing

to send $10 to his ministry each month. And back then, $10
seemed like $10,000. It was a lot of money, but I knew it was
something we had to do.

I noticed that the anointing to lay hands on the sick began
to manifest in my life not
even a week after Gloria
and I had become partners
with Dr. Roberts' ministry.
The same healing anoint-
ing on Oral Roberts began
working in me.

> *The same healing anointing on* **Oral Roberts** *began working in me.*

When I first noticed
this, it caught me by surprise. Because the mind-set I had
grown up with in church was, "You never know when God
might decide to anoint somebody. About every 100 years, or
so, He might need another Billy Graham or Oral Roberts, so
he dumps a load on someone...but you just never know who
or when."

In this case, however, there was no mystery. It was a
deliberate act on my part—and God's.

If you think about it, that's not how God called and
anointed anyone in the Bible anyway. There was never any
uncertainty about how someone received and operated in
His power. Like everything else in His kingdom, it worked
according to the principle of sowing and reaping.

For instance, Joshua spent 40 years of his life at the side
of Moses. Then, when Moses passed away, Joshua stepped
into a higher level of anointing than what even Moses had
known. Joshua reaped what he sowed, and he sowed walking
in a covenant relationship, or communion, with Moses.

Elisha did the same thing. He gave up his own lifestyle
to stay as close to the prophet Elijah as he could. They were
connected. And when Elijah left this earth, Elisha received a

> *God's plan is the same today.*

double portion of Elijah's anointing. This process of transferring or imparting God's anointing was no different in the days of the New Testament.

When Jesus called His disciples out one by one, He told them, "Come, follow Me!" They responded by joining with Him. They made a divine connection by becoming partners in His ministry. As a result, the same anointing that flowed through His life and ministry flowed through theirs.

Now, when Jesus ascended into heaven, His disciples were obviously no longer connected with Him physically. But as we said earlier, God sent the Holy Spirit. Suddenly, the disciples could be connected to Jesus in spirit by being born again of God's Spirit and being baptized in His Anointing.

With this divine connection in place, soon, everywhere the disciples went, new believers were drawn to them and were now becoming their partners in the gospel. People supported their ministries and churches in every way possible, thereby allowing all the anointings and giftings of the apostle, prophet, evangelist, pastor and teacher to flow freely, back and forth among all of them.

At last, the plan God had established before the foundation of the world was in full swing. And the Church—the Body of anointed ones—was as Paul described: "fitly joined together and compacted by that which every joint supplieth, according to the effectual working in the measure of every part..." (Ephesians 4:16). ❧

The Devil's Nightmare

God's plan is the same today.

No matter what your vocation is, God wants every gifting and anointing of the apostle, prophet, evangelist, pastor and teacher alive and active in your life—just the same as He does in every minister of the gospel.

Think about it. Jesus is the Vine and we are His branches. The vine and branches are connected to each other. They are one. That means *all* the branches—not just a few—have access to the sap that is in the vine. The same sap that flows through the vine flows through all its branches.

There is one problem to all this, however.

You see, the devil's biggest nightmare is the Church completely unified and flowing in that fullness of Jesus' anointings. That's why he has been doing everything he can for centuries to keep the Body of Christ—the Body of God's anointed ones—divided and disconnected from one another. To do so renders us powerless.

In the end, however, we know the devil will fail.

But that does not mean we don't have a major part in bringing the plan of God to pass.

Rather, that's all the more reason we must find out where and how God wants us plugged into the local church. The local church is where our spiritual life is rooted and grounded. That means we need to ask God where He wants us to settle down and take root—where He wants us to connect.

Once He tells us, we need to get in that local church and pour our lives into it...as though *we* were the pastor.

Then, we must find out which ministries God wants us to join in covenant partnership.

Jesus commissioned each of us to "...Go ye into all the world, and preach the gospel to every creature" (Mark 16:15). If we personally cannot go, then it's our responsibility to send someone else.

God will show us the ministries with which we need to connect. And when He does, we need to invest our lives and resources into them. We need to do whatever He tells us to do, and do it with the heart of an apostle, prophet, evangelist, pastor and teacher.

Once we take these steps toward covenant partnership, we can expect every anointing and gifting of Jesus to begin flowing through our lives—and when that happens, the Church will finally see real power and real manifestation of God's glory in this earth.

Study Questions

(1) What is the primary reason why the Church has seemed "powerless" in recent years? THE Body of God ANOinTED ONES divide and disCONNECTED FROM ONE ANOTHER

(2) What should be the "motive" for the Church coming together? Why do we "fellowship"? (See Philippians 1:3-5.) I thANK my God EVERytime I RememBeR you IN All my pRAyeRS foR All of you I AlwAys pRAy with Joy BecAuse of youR PARtneRship in the Gospel from The first dAy until Now.

(3) What is the "advantage" that we as the Church have today? (See Ephesians 4:7.) Unto EveRy one of us IS GiveN GRAce AccoRding to the meAsuRe of the Gift of ChRisT

(4) What is the "anointing"? (See Isaiah 10.)

Study Questions

(5) By what means can you expect the anointing of the "fivefold ministry" to flow through your life and ministry? _____

_____

_____

_____

_____

(6) Does the flow of a prophet's anointing in your life require an act on God's part, your part, or both? Explain using one example of an Old Testament prophet. _____

_____

_____

_____

_____

_____

(7) What are the two ways (points of contact) each believer should be "connected" through covenant partnership? Explain the believer's role in each case. _____

_____

_____

_____

_____

_____

_____

Study Notes

_____

_____

_____

_____

_____

_____

_____

_____

_____

_____

_____

_____

_____

_____

_____

_____

_____

_____

_____

_____

_____

_____

_____

_____

_____

*"Unto every one of us is given grace [anointing]
according to the measure of the gift of Christ [the anointing]."*
Ephesians 4:7

2

"He that receiveth a prophet in the name of a prophet shall receive a prophet's reward; and he that receiveth a righteous man in the name of a righteous man shall receive a righteous man's reward. And whosoever shall give to drink unto one of these little ones a cup of cold water only in the name of a disciple, verily I say unto you, he shall in no wise lose his reward."

Matthew 10:41-42

CHAPTER TWO
Receiving a Prophet's Reward

There Are Earthly and Heavenly Rewards for Making Covenant Connections

Left Behind—But
Not Left Out

As we've already seen, partnership is a system designed by God to dramatically increase the abilities, resources and rewards of every believer.

Up to now, we have seen the overall scope of God's plan and purpose for partnership in our lives, particularly how it relates to the anointing. But now it's time for us to direct our study toward the application of partnership...how we can apply it in the "material" or "natural" realm of life, as well as the "spiritual" realm.

Contrary to what most people probably think, *partnership* is not a marketing strategy designed to raise money—not when it comes to partnership in ministry.

No, the kind of partnership we're talking about is a holy ordinance established by God. It

> *Partnership is a holy ordinance established by God.*

dates back to the early days of Israel in the Old Testament, on through the New Testament, and continues today.

One of the key principles of partnership was *officially* established and recognized as an ordinance of God in the days just prior to David's becoming king over Israel.

In 1 Samuel 30, we find David and his band of 600 warriors in hot pursuit of the Amalekites who had plundered their homes and taken their families captive.

In order to overtake their enemy, David's men had embarked on a grueling military maneuver known as a forced march—moving troops and equipment as far and as fast as possible, while remaining battle-ready at all times. It was tough, and by the time David and his men reached the brook Besor, 200 of them were too exhausted to go any farther.

So, David instructed the weary ones to remain behind and guard the supplies, while he and the rest of the troops pressed on.

In the end, David and his men overtook the Amalekites, totally defeating them, recovering all their wives, children and possessions, and plundering all that belonged to the Amalekites.

When David and the 400 soldiers returned to camp at the brook Besor, they arrived with all the spoils of war. But when it came time to divide all those spoils among the men, some of the 400 who had gone on to fight did not want to share with the 200 who had stayed behind.

"...Because they went not with us, we will not give them aught of the spoil that we have recovered," they said (1 Samuel 30:22).

It was at that crucial moment that David—a man after God's own heart—officially established the principle of partnership. For he told the men: "Ye shall not do so, my brethren, with that which the Lord hath given us...but as his part is that goeth down to the battle, so shall his part be that tarrieth by the stuff: they shall part alike. And it was so from that day forward, that he made it a statute and an ordinance for Israel unto this day" (verses 23-25).

Now, you may be thinking that an ancient ordinance like this does not mean much to you today. But it does. You are a soldier in God's army, just like David's men were. You are on a mission to occupy this earth and enforce the devil's defeat until Jesus returns.

Maybe you're on the frontlines of battle as an apostle, prophet, evangelist, pastor or teacher. Or, maybe you're back at the camp watching over the "stuff."

Either way, there are rewards for you.

The point is, if you are "back at the camp"—if you are in partnership with a minister of the gospel who is doing the work of God out on the frontlines, and you're fighting alongside him or her through prayer and through your finances—God makes no distinction between the two of you.

You are guaranteed eternal rewards for every person born again, healed and delivered through that ministry, just the same as the man or woman who is fulfilling the office of apostle, prophet, evangelist, pastor or teacher.

In 36 years of ministry, Kenneth Copeland Ministries has seen millions of people come into the kingdom of God. But in heaven's accounting system, Gloria and I are not the only ones who receive credit for all those souls. As God sees it, the Partners of Kenneth Copeland Ministries receive credit for those precious souls as well. And it all goes back to the ordinance that David proclaimed before man and God.

Partnership Has Its Benefits

It's interesting to note that when Jesus launched His 12 disciples into ministry, He made a point to teach them this principle concerning the "rewards" of partnership. We find Him explaining it to them in Matthew 10:40-42:

> He that receiveth you receiveth me, and he
> that receiveth me receiveth him that sent me.
> He that receiveth a prophet in the name of a
> prophet shall receive a prophet's reward; and he
> that receiveth a righteous man in the name of a

righteous man shall receive a righteous man's reward. And whosoever shall give to drink unto one of these little ones a cup of cold water only in the name of a disciple, verily I say unto you, he shall in no wise lose his reward.

It would be sufficiently exciting if the rewards we received from our partnership in God's work were strictly heavenly rewards. But, praise God, they're not.

There are rewards for you.

The earthly aspect to this reward system of partnership is actually one of God's ways of providing us blessings so great that we could never muster up enough faith to receive them on our own.

We see an example of this in 2 Kings 4 where we find the account of a Shunammite woman who decided to support the ministry of the prophet Elisha. She was so determined to be a partner in his work that one day when he was passing by, she "constrained him to eat bread" (verse 8).

In other words, this woman just would not take no for an answer. She insisted that Elisha stay for dinner. But she didn't stop with that.

The Shunammite woman and her husband built a special room onto their house so Elisha could have a place to stay whenever he was in town.

In return for their partnership in his ministry, Elisha told his servant Gehazi, "Go find out what we can do for this woman. Find out what she wants."

So, Gehazi went and checked out the situation, then came back and gave Elisha his report: "...Verily she hath no child, and her husband is old" (2 Kings 4:14).

With that, Elisha instructed Gehazi: "...Call her. And when he [Gehazi] had called her, she stood in the door. And [Elisha] said, About this season, according to the time of life, thou shalt embrace a son. And she said, Nay, my lord, thou man of God, do not lie unto thine handmaid" (verses 15-16).

Obviously the woman did not have the faith to believe God for a child because when Elisha told her she would bear a son, she said, "No way! You may be a prophet, but you cannot be telling me the truth!" Having a child was beyond what she could ask or think.

> *Gloria and I encourage our Partners to draw purposefully on the faith in our lives and ministry.*

On the other hand, Elisha had no trouble believing for this woman to conceive and deliver a son. Since she was due a reward and they were in partnership with one another, he simply released his faith on her behalf—and by the next year, she had a baby boy in her arms.

Over the years, Gloria and I have encouraged our Partners to draw purposefully on the faith in our lives and ministry. We've spent the past 36 years developing it. We want Partners to draw on our faith to their advantage. We want them to use it to help them accomplish those "faith projects" they encountered in life that seemed just a little more than what they could believe God for on their own. And time and time again, we've seen our Partners get results...their rightful *earthly* rewards.

Maybe you are facing what seems to be a MOUNTAIN of debt. Maybe it's more than what you think your faith can handle.

Just tap into one of the many earthly privileges of partnership. Draw on the faith that Gloria and I have for supernatural debt reduction. The first thing we stepped out to believe God for when we started this ministry in 1967 was $24,000 worth of debt to be eliminated. Before the end of the year, thank God, it was totally removed from our lives. Years later we were faced with a ministry deficit of six million. Once again faith was the victory that overcame the world.

In fact, Gloria and I and our staff have to believe for millions of dollars every month for the various outreaches of this ministry. And I assure you that we have the faith for it. ✍

What You Need...
When You Need It

In the first chapter of this book, we found out from the Apostle Paul how the grace, or *anointing,* that is on the men and women in the fivefold ministry offices can be transferred to any believer through partnership.

That means the anointings and giftings that God has placed in and on Gloria and me for ministry are available to you as our Partners.

But how can you apply that in practical terms, given that you may be a car salesman, a schoolteacher, a business owner or a homemaker?

Well, going back to Paul's great revelation concerning partnership in ministry, let's take another look at what he wrote to his partners in Philippians 1:3-7:

> I thank my God upon every remembrance of you,
> always in every prayer of mine for you all making
> request with joy, for your fellowship [or partnership]
> in the gospel from the first day until now; being

confident of this very thing, that he which hath begun
a good work in you will perform it until the day of
Jesus Christ: Even as it is meet for me to think this of
you all, because I have you in my heart; inasmuch as
both in my bonds, and in the defence and confirmation of the gospel, ye all are partakers of my grace.

Notice in that last phrase Paul said, Ye are "partakers
of my grace." He did not say, *"God's* grace." He said,
"My grace."

In other words, Paul was saying, "As my partners, you share
in the anointing God has given
me to carry out my ministry."

God intended for the signs and wonders of His Spirit to be the benefit of unbelievers.

To understand just how signif-
icant that statement is, take the
time to read through some of
Paul's letters and see the other
comments he makes about grace,
or anointing. He makes statements
such as: "By the grace [anointing]
of God I am what I am...I laboured more abundantly than they
all: yet not I, but the grace [anointing] of God which was with
me" (1 Corinthians 15:10).

So, as we concluded in the first chapter, Paul was literally
telling the Philippians that, as his partners, the same anointings that were on him as an apostle had become available to
them for ministry.

When I first stepped out into the ministry years ago, the
Lord began talking to me about partnership and He told me,
*Kenneth, I'm not raising up churches just to give you boys a
place to preach. I'm raising them up to meet the needs of My
people: The anointing is on you for them.*

After He said that, I also began to realize that God did

not give the Body of Christ the gifts of the Spirit for us to spend on ourselves. He gave us His Word to get our healing and health, to deliver us out of debt and lack and into financial prosperity and abundance. He gave us His Word for anything and everything we need.

On the other hand, God gave the gifts of His Spirit to the Church so we could in turn minister to a lost, hurting, broke, sick, dying, going-to-hell world. He intended for the signs and wonders of His Spirit to be for the benefit of unbelievers.

The signs and wonders were to draw lost people into the Church, and we were anointed by God to minister His Word and His Anointing to them. That was His plan.

So, whether you are a lawyer, mechanic, farmer or student, you are still called to witness to people, pray for them and minister to them as you go about your daily affairs. And the more of the Anointing of God you have available to you, the more effectively you will be able to do it.

But now, understand that this works both ways.

When you become partners with a ministry, the mechanic anointing, the lawyer anointing, or whatever anointing that is on you for your profession, becomes available to that ministry. That way, none of us is lacking on any front—and I guarantee you that, where this ministry is concerned, there are plenty of times we need the mechanic anointing, the lawyer anointing and so forth.

My point is, each one of us in the Body of Christ can—and should—have the full scope of God's anointing alive and active in our daily lives, whether it's in the sense of doing our job or ministering to a neighbor.

Each of us can also enjoy the prophet's reward—all the benefits of being associated with ministries—by joining our faith together to receive exceeding abundantly above all we ask or think. ~❧

I am truly convinced that it was this "prophet's reward" that Paul had in mind when, in closing his letter to his Philippian partners, he said, "My God [the One that anointed me] shall supply all your need according to his riches in glory by Christ Jesus" (Philippians 4:19).

No matter how you look at it, this deal is too good to pass up. So don't!

Determine in your heart, and make a quality decision in your mind that you will begin making that draw of faith on the anointings and giftings God has placed in and on Gloria and me and this ministry.

Stay connected...and receive the prophet's reward!

❧ S t u d y Q u e s t i o n s ❧

*(1) Who "officially" established the principle of partnership? (See 1 Samuel 30.)*_____

_____

_____

_____

(2) What distinctions does God make between "frontline" believers/ministers and those who remain back at the "camp"? And what is the difference between the "mission" of these two groups?

_____

_____

_____

_____

*(3) What phrase did Jesus use to describe the benefit of partnership? (See Matthew 10:41.)*_____

_____

_____

_____

_____

(4) What two things (one earthly and one spiritual) did the Shunammite woman lack? (See 2 Kings 4:14-16.) _____

_____

_____

_____

Study Questions

(5) List three "earthly" and three "spiritual" benefits you see that you could receive through your partnership with Kenneth Copeland Ministries. ___

_____

_____

_____

_____

(6) How do you partake of the grace that is in/on a minister of the gospel? (See Philippians 1:3-7.) _____

_____

_____

_____

_____

(7) Who did God primarily intend to receive benefit from the gifts of the Spirit? Explain. _____

_____

_____

_____

_____

(8) What is one way God can "supply all your need"? _____

_____

_____

_____

_____

_____

Study Notes

"...As his part is that goeth down to the battle, so shall his part be that tarrieth by the stuff: they shall part alike."

1 Samuel 30:24

3

"Jesus took the loaves; and
when he had given thanks, he
distributed to the disciples, and
the disciples to them that were
set down; and likewise of the fishes
as much as they would. When they
were filled, he said unto his disciples,
Gather up the fragments that remain,
that nothing be lost. Therefore they
gathered them together, and filled
twelve baskets with the fragments...."

John 6:11-13

CHAPTER THREE
Getting in Touch With the Anointing of Increase

Seedtime and Harvest Is the Key to Increase

Sowing and Reaping—
It's as Old as Dirt

For centuries the Church has been riddled with ungodly ideas concerning prosperity.

In fact, the Body of Christ has been dominated by the world's financial system for so long that in many places people are being taught the world's ways of doing business—when God has had little or nothing to do with them.

The problem has been that we brought the world's systems and the world's ways over into the Church instead of taking God's ways into the world.

But now all that is changing. It must change.

We've come to the end of 2,000 years since Jesus' birth into this earth. That's 2,000 years' worth of gospel that has been sown into this world, and now it's harvest time. And you and I are the ones who are called by God to reap that harvest.

How?

Through *partnership.*

As we saw in the last chapter, partnership has its benefits. We discovered that there are actually rewards for making covenant connections where God leads us—*earthly* rewards, as well as *heavenly* ones.

In this chapter we are going to explore another of those rewards, or benefits, of partnership—"the anointing of increase." It is a reward that most certainly is grounded in God's principles of supernatural increase in this material world. But it is also a principle founded on the concept of sowing a seed twice—or, twice-sown seed.

Therefore, before we get into the *reaping* side of this principle, I want to make sure you have a solid foundation and understanding of the *sowing* side of it. After all, you cannot reap...unless you sow. And the best place to begin to look for insight and understanding about sowing and reaping is "in the beginning"—the Genesis account of it.

Genesis 8:20-22 tells us what God first had to say about sowing and reaping:

> Noah builded an altar unto the Lord; and took of every clean beast, and of every clean fowl, and offered burnt offerings on the altar. And the Lord smelled a sweet savour; and the Lord said in his heart, I will not again curse the ground any more for man's sake; for the imagination of man's heart is evil from his youth; neither will I again smite any more every thing living, as I have done. While the earth remaineth, seedtime and harvest, and cold and heat, and summer and winter, and day and night shall not cease.

Notice that last verse: "While the earth remaineth, seedtime and harvest...shall not cease."

God was saying, *Count on seedtime and harvest being around for a while.*

And it has.

But what exactly does that mean to us today?

And how does it relate to our being Partners?

To answer those questions, let's begin by examining the word *seedtime*. It is a compound word that is defined as "the season for planting seeds." If you analyze it, particularly in the context of this passage, it is telling us that with everything we sow there's always a time of planting, a time of growing and a time of harvesting.

Jesus followed through with this concept of seedtime—growing time—in the New Testament when His apostles

approached Him about increasing their faith. We read about it
in Luke 17:5-6: "The apostles said unto the Lord, Increase
our faith. And the Lord said, If ye had faith as a grain of mus-
tard seed, ye might say unto this sycamine tree, Be thou
plucked up by the root, and be thou planted in the sea; and it
should obey you."

The apostles went to Jesus because they wanted their
faith to increase, or grow. He, in turn, explained that their
faith was like a seed. If
they would plant it, it
would grow.

In other words, faith
follows the law of seedtime
and harvest. It must be
planted...and it must be
allowed to grow.

> *You and I are
> the ones who are
> called by God to
> reap the harvest.*

Finally, the Apostle Paul gives us further insight into
sowing and reaping in Galatians 6:7-8, which says this: "Be
not deceived; God is not mocked: for whatsoever a man
soweth, that shall he also reap. For he that soweth to his flesh
shall of the flesh reap corruption; but he that soweth to the
Spirit shall of the Spirit reap life everlasting."

The bottom line is that the law of sowing and reaping is a
kingdom law which governs the earth and all material matter,
natural and spiritual.

So, when you take this basic, yet all-encompassing law
of kingdom economics and apply it to this compressed, nar-
row band of time in which we now live as people of the end
times—a time when 6,000 years' worth of God's promises are
exploding into fulfillment all over this earth—that's when
things really begin to get interesting. ✌

Pressed for Time

Have you ever noticed how we seem to be a generation of people who are always in a hurry and forever running out of time?

Though we have all the technology to do anything and everything faster than ever before, we're always out of time. I can tell you why.

It's because...we're out of time!

Amos 9:13 explains our dilemma: "Behold, the days come, saith the Lord, that the plowman shall overtake the reaper, and the treader of grapes him that soweth seed...."

> *Faith follows the law of seedtime and harvest. It must be planted...and it must be allowed to grow.*

This is a picture and prophecy of that end-time harvest for which we have all been praying and looking. But take note what is really happening in this verse—and, again, the key is growing time.

How much *growing time* do you think is involved when a farmer is out in the field, walking a couple of feet behind the guy driving the plow, poking grape seeds in the ground...and then just a few steps behind him is the fellow who is pulling ripe grapes off a mature vine?

I would say the growing time—the span of time from seed to ripe fruit—is only a matter of seconds. But that's not even what this scripture is emphasizing.

This verse is actually drawing attention to the fact that the plowman, the planter, the reaper and the winemaker are all catching up to one another and passing each other, to the point that you cannot tell which one is which.

Is it beginning to seem a little impossible?

Well, in the natural realm it is. But let's find out more about this principle of growing time, and how supernatural growing time relates to our end-time harvest and partnership.

Let's focus the rest of our study on John 6:5-13, and start by reading verses 5-9:

> When Jesus then lifted up his eyes, and saw a great company come unto him, he saith unto Philip, Whence shall we buy bread, that these may eat? And this he said to prove him: for he himself knew what he would do. Philip answered him, Two hundred pennyworth of bread is not sufficient for them, that every one of them may take a little. One of his disciples, Andrew, Simon Peter's brother, saith unto him, There is a lad here, which hath five barley loaves, and two small fishes: but what are they among so many?

Before we read the rest of the passage, I want to stop here and examine these verses so we can get a good idea of what's really happening—what Jesus is saying and how His disciples are responding.

When Jesus looked up and saw the multitude coming, He asked Philip, "Where are we going to buy bread for all these people?"

Jesus already knew the answer, but He asked anyway, because—as *The Amplified Bible* says—He wanted to "test" Philip. He wanted to get Philip's attention and make him think. And I am convinced that Philip's answer is why Jesus did what He did.

You see, Jesus was—and is—aware of the fact that the way you and I learn is through communication. That is to say, we never really know what we believe until we start hearing our own mouths say it. We may think we have a pretty good handle on some things. But until the pressure gets turned up to the point where words and thoughts start jumping out of our mouths, we never really know what is deep inside.

Jesus once said, "…Out of the abundance of the heart the mouth speaketh" (Matthew 12:34).

This passage in John leaves no question as to what Philip had in his heart and on his mind that day. *Little.* He had *little* on his mind.

In fact, faced with all those hungry people, little was the biggest thing in Philip's eyes. And by that I mean, all he could see at that moment was the problem...

How are we going to feed all these folks?

Just getting a few crumbs into these people's hands was far bigger than any answer he could imagine. ᴄ᠑

Seed for the Need

With little more than a few crumbs to offer thousands of hungry people, Philip stepped aside and along came Andrew, who got in on the test, too.

Let's see if he does any better (John 6:8-9): "One of his disciples, Andrew, Simon Peter's brother, saith unto him, There is a lad here, which hath five barley loaves, and two small fishes…."

Now, at first, Andrew did pretty well. He had heard the Spirit of God enough to realize the answer. But Andrew's problem came when he allowed his own reasoning to talk him out of the answer.

Andrew started out in the right direction, but look where he ended up: "There is a lad here, which hath five barley loaves, and two small fishes: but what are they among so many?"

His image of the supply turned into crumbs, just like Philip's.

I suspect Andrew never realized that he had tapped into the answer to Jesus' question. Yet, I believe he picked up on it from the Spirit of God.

Why else would he bring that little boy with a basket of lunch to Jesus?

In the end, both Philip and Andrew allowed the size of the problem and their own reasoning to block their view of the answer, though it was standing beside them the whole time, staring them in the face.

> *Andrew's problem came when he allowed his own reasoning to talk him out of the answer.*

But now, let's watch carefully how Jesus handles this situation. Let's pick up with the rest of this passage in John 6:10-13:

> And Jesus said, Make the men sit down. Now there was much grass in the place. So the men sat down, in number about five thousand. And Jesus took the loaves; and when he had given thanks, he distributed to the disciples, and the disciples to them that were set down; and likewise of the fishes as much as they would. When they were filled, he said unto his disciples, Gather up the fragments that remain, that nothing be lost. Therefore they gathered them together, and filled twelve baskets with the fragments of the five barley loaves, which remained over and above unto them that had eaten.

On that day, heaven has it recorded that a little boy fed 5,000 men and all their families with two small fish and five loaves of bread. Certainly, Jesus performed the miracle and distributed the food. But it was not His seed to sow until that lad walked up and handed Him his lunch.

Matthew 14 records the same event, and in verse 19 we read how Jesus took the seed—the bread and fish—gave thanks for it, blessed it, broke it and gave it to His disciples. Before Jesus did all this, however, He told the disciples, "Bring them hither to me" (verse 18).

Why do you suppose Jesus told the disciples to give Him the bread and fish?

Couldn't He just as easily have said, "Hold them up and let Me bless them?"

The reason Jesus wanted to *handle the seed* was because of the anointing of increase.

Producing Optimum Results

Today, there is an anointing of *increase* that is literally and figuratively in the hands of the ministers of the gospel—just as it was present in Jesus' hands the day He fed a multitude of hungry people with two small fish and five loaves of bread.

We see this anointing for increase in the hands of God's ministry throughout the Bible. That's why God instructed Israel in the Old Testament, and Christians in the New Testament, to bring all their tithes, offerings and goods into the ministry.

God's way is for material goods to come into the ministry—for the ministry to receive them, handle them, bless them and distribute them, or sow them. Then His plan is for those goods to go out, multiplied in greater number than when they came in.

That's the anointing of increase. It's the same anointing we find described in 2 Corinthians 9:10: "Now he that ministereth seed to the sower both minister bread for your food, and multiply your seed sown, and increase the fruits of your righteousness."

So when the boy sowed seed into Jesus' ministry, Jesus received it, applied His anointing of increase to it, then turned around and sowed it into His disciples and the multitude. As the anointing of increase in and on Jesus hit that boy's seed, not only did it cause the seed to multiply, but it also did something supernatural to the growing time.

> *Today, there is an anointing of increase that is in the hands of the ministers of the gospel.*

Optimum results were produced in minimal time. The seed's growing time was compressed to the point that the seed multiplied, grew and produced fruit as fast as the people could eat it. Harvest was produced within moments, which takes us back to Amos 9:13: "The plowman shall overtake the reaper, and the treader of grapes him that soweth seed...."

But the story did not end there.

After those 20,000 people had eaten and were full, Jesus told His disciples to "gather up the fragments that remain, that nothing be lost."

Was Jesus being greedy?

No. Those 12 baskets of leftovers belonged to that boy, and Jesus was just making sure He did not lose any of the boy's harvest—and that was just his immediate harvest from having sown directly into Jesus' ministry.

The fulfillment of this boy's harvest, the fulfillment of God's obligation to him, was the fruit from seeds multiplied and sown into the lives of 20,000 people.

In one afternoon he fed thousands of people—including Jesus—and had enough seed to last a lifetime.

My friend, the twice-sown seed is where we as the Body of Christ need to learn to exercise our faith and keep our expectancy.

Thinking *little* like Philip will not bring in the end-time harvest that's facing us. Only God's way of thinking will do—and His way is "pressed down, and shaken together, and running over" (Luke 6:38).

God did not create a corncob with one kernel of corn on it. He created a corncob with an abundance of kernels on it. And all creation is designed the same way.

We've entered an era in which 2,000 years' worth of gospel seed planted is coming up a hundredfold. It's a time in which the plowmen and reapers are passing each other until you cannot tell which is which.

So before we leave this place, let's get in on God's system of economics and get a net-breaking, boat-sinking load of souls through our partnership...and the supernatural flow of God's anointing of increase.

Study Questions

(1) What principle (related to your prosperity) did God institute in Genesis 8:22? _____

_____

_____

_____

_____

(2) Give an expanded definition of "seedtime." _____

_____

_____

_____

_____

(3) What "spiritual" application did Jesus make to "seedtime" in Luke 17:5-6? _____

_____

_____

_____

_____

(4) What insight to "seedtime" does Paul offer in Galations 6:7-8? ___

_____

_____

_____

_____

_____

Study Questions

(5) Write out the Old Testament scripture that describes the end-time harvest. _____

_____

_____

_____

_____

(6) How is it possible to sow a "seed" twice? (See John 6:9-13.) _____

_____

_____

_____

_____

(7) At what point was the "anointing of increase" applied to the lad's loaves and fishes? (See John 6:11.) _____

_____

_____

_____

_____

(8) Apply the "twice-sown seed" principle to your relationship with Kenneth Copeland Ministries (explain how the process would work in your life). _____

_____

_____

_____

_____

Study Notes

_____

_____

_____

_____

_____

_____

_____

_____

_____

_____

_____

_____

_____

_____

_____

_____

_____

_____

_____

_____

_____

_____

*"Behold, the days come, saith the Lord, that the plowman
shall overtake the reaper, and the treader of grapes
him that soweth seed...."*
Amos 9:13

4

"Being confident of this very thing, that he which hath begun a good work in you will perform it until the day of Jesus Christ: Even as it is meet for me to think this of you all, because I have you in my heart; inasmuch as both in my bonds, and in the defence and confirmation of the gospel, ye all are partakers of my grace."

Philippians 1:6-7

CHAPTER FOUR
In Times of Need...
We Need Each Other

Partnership Is a
Two-Way Exchange of
God's Grace and Power

Knocking the Wind Out of Disaster

Several years ago a line of tornadoes ripped across Central Texas, causing massive destruction.

One tornado in particular hit a little town and nearly wiped it out—and I don't say that just as a figure of speech. Several blocks of houses, including some businesses, were literally flattened.

Meteorologists tracking the tornado said it was more than half a mile wide and had surface winds of more than 250 miles per hour.

When any sort of national disaster like this happens, one of the first things our staff at Kenneth Copeland Ministries does is pray. Then we begin checking our lists and calling to find out if we have any Partners who have been affected by the disaster.

We make every effort to find out what we can do to help our Partners, as well as their communities.

In this case, we learned that we had a Partner right in the middle of that tornado's path of destruction.

> *We make every effort to find out what we can do to help our Partners, as well as their communities.*

When we finally got a call through to him, he said, "Tell Kenneth and Gloria we're all right. That tornado got within half a block of our house but we took authority over it. We just started talking to it, and it went around us and on to downtown where it wiped out all the others."

Thank God we have His Word and His Anointing. But

thank God that we also have each other. We need each other. We need each other's faith and prayers.

That's why it is so important for us to be connected with one another in partnership. Our individual anointings and prayers of faith flowing together are far more powerful than any one of us alone could ever be. And they are certainly more powerful than any storm the devil might throw our way—which is how God intended it to be.

Gloria and I are honored to have more than 240,000 Partners around the world—and soon to be a million—that's anointed, praying, believing Partners.

Like you, these are believers who have joined their faith and their love with Gloria's and mine and our staff's. They are committed to support this ministry in every way the Spirit of God leads them.

I don't mind telling you that it is a great source of joy and strength just knowing that all our Partners are out there standing strong with us, wherever we might be in the world, facing whatever storms we might have to face.

> *It is a great source of joy and strength just to know that all our Partners are out there standing strong with us.*

After all, it takes far more than what Gloria and I have in order to get this message of victory in Jesus into the hands of God's people.

For the past 36 years of ministry, Gloria and I have been like the Apostle Paul, who—when he wrote to *his* partners—said:

I thank my God in all my remembrance of you.
In every prayer of mine I always make my entreaty

and petition for you all with joy (delight). [I thank
my God] for your fellowship (your sympathetic
cooperation and contributions and partnership)
in advancing the good news (the Gospel) from the
first day [you heard it] until now (Philippians 1:3-5,
The Amplified Bible).

The list of KCM Partners is long. But each name on that
list represents a real, flesh-and-blood, Holy Ghost-anointed
person who is in covenant with us—as well as with each
other—helping us take the uncompromised Word of God to
the nations.

Consequently, Gloria and I hold these precious souls
in our hearts every moment of every day. Not a day goes by
that we don't pray for our Partners, using a list of specific
scriptures that the Lord has given us to pray and believe on
their behalf.

When Paul wrote this letter to his partners in Philippi, he
was not just scratching out some nice words to make them
feel all warm and good.

He was explaining important spiritual principles where
ministry was concerned. He was explaining the exchange,
or two-way flow, of God's grace and power in partnerships
established for the sake of ministry.

And while prayer is a major part of this partnership
exchange, Paul was saying that there was even more being
transferred in their exchange. We read about it in what is now
a familiar passage to us about partnership:

Being confident of this very thing, that he which
hath begun a good work in you will perform it until
the day of Jesus Christ: Even as it is meet [able] for
me to think this of you all, because I have you in my

heart; inasmuch as both in my bonds, and in the defence and confirmation of the gospel, ye all are partakers of my grace (Philippians 1:6-7).

As we've already seen, Paul was telling his partners, "Hey, we're in this together. And the grace—or anointings—that God put on me, He has put on you by having joined us together. So, expect every anointing and blessing that I have operating in my life to operate in yours as well!"

Think of that verse in light of our KCM Partner standing outside his house with a half-mile-wide tornado half a block away.

There is no telling how many times I prayed for that one Partner as I lifted my hands toward heaven and said, "Father, I pray for my Partners today…," and then went through all the scriptures I pray, and ended by praying in other tongues.

In fact, one of the scriptures I pray for my Partners in Psalm 91 says, "A thousand shall fall at thy side, and ten thousand at thy right hand; but it shall not come nigh thee" (verse 7).

Do you see the benefit of that scripture prayed for this man and his home?

Well, it doesn't stop there!

Consider the other 240,000 Partners around the world praying for this man through the power of being divinely connected.

Consider the KCM staff around the world praying for this man, agreeing and joining their faith with scriptures such as:

Psalm 23:4: "Yea, though I walk through the valley of the shadow of death, I will fear no evil: for thou art with me…."

Psalm 103:4: "Who redeemeth thy life from destruction…."

Isaiah 54:17: "No weapon that is formed against thee shall prosper…."

Now, imagine that tornado whirling itself down our Partner's street, but suddenly having to go around a particular house because of the 240,000-strong prayers, anointings and faith standing in its way.

I guarantee you that partnership—corporate prayers, corporate anointings and corporate faith—is what turned a storm of that magnitude away.

So it's important to understand that in covenant partnership, when you pray for Gloria and me, you are praying for a man in Central Texas. And when he prays for Gloria and me, he is praying for you. And on and on it goes...around the world.

That is the exchange and flow of prayer and anointing through partnership. That's the strength of it. That's how God designed it. It is partaking of each other's grace.

Behind Every Good Preacher...

As we study the wealth of spiritual instruction Paul left behind in his writings to his New Testament partners, I believe there is a subtle mind-set from which we must guard ourselves. I say subtle; yet, over centuries it is a mind-set that has developed into a stronghold of religious tradition.

The mind-set I'm referring to is the one that says, "Oh sure, Brother Copeland, it's nice to think we can partake of each other's grace. But, let's face it, that was the Apostle Paul—handpicked by Jesus Himself. I can't expect that kind of power to flow through my life...I'm not the Apostle Paul."

In other words, we must guard against putting Paul—or any other Church leader, for that matter—up on a spiritual pedestal and labeling his life and ministry as "unrealistic for me today."

Let me show you what I mean.

Let's pick up with Paul's letter to his partners in Philippi by reading Philippians 1:19-20:

> For I know that this shall turn to my salvation
> through your prayer, and the supply of the Spirit
> of Jesus Christ [the Anointed One], according to
> my earnest expectation and my hope, that in nothing
> I shall be ashamed, but that with all boldness, as
> always, so now also Christ [the Anointed One and
> His Anointing] shall be magnified in my body,
> whether it be by life, or by death.

It's obvious that Paul earnestly expected his partners to pray and stand with him, so he could do what he had been called by God to do. He expected his partners to covenant with him, to join with him and undergird him with prayer. It was those prayers that were so vital to Paul's ministry. They were his connection to an even greater supply of the Spirit—a greater supply of anointing necessary to get the job done. The prayers of Paul's partners were his connection to their corporate anointings.

Consequently, if Paul's partners did not pray and daily hold him up, as he was them, then there was a definite possibility that failure could be at his doorstep. The exchange or flow of prayer and anointing would be hindered.

That's right. Paul's ministry could have actually failed. And where would that have left us today?

In writing to the church at Philippi, Paul basically acknowledged: "Without your prayers and support, I will be ashamed before God because I won't be able to complete all that I am supposed to do. By myself I will fall short."

To prove even further Paul's reliance upon the prayers and support of his partners, let's take one aspect of Paul's ministry to see how this partnership exchange applies—his boldness.

The prayers of Paul's partners were his connection to their corporate anointings.

When we think of the Apostle Paul, we might often think of the boldness demonstrated throughout his life and ministry. He was a very bold man. There were times when he would get right up in the faces of kings and high officials, point his finger at them and say, "You will not get away with this!"

And they didn't.

We can certainly attribute Paul's boldness to his keen awareness of his position of authority as a born-again child of God in the Anointed Jesus. Nevertheless, there was something uncommon about his boldness.

Where did he get such boldness?

Let's answer that question by reading a portion of a letter Paul wrote to another group of partners. It's found in Ephesians 6:10-20:

> Finally, my brethren, be strong in the Lord, and in
> the power of his might. Put on the whole armour of
> God, that ye may be able to stand against the wiles
> of the devil. For we wrestle not against flesh and
> blood, but against principalities, against powers,
> against the rulers of the darkness of this world,

against spiritual wickedness in high places. Wherefore take unto you the whole armour of God, that ye may be able to withstand in the evil day, and having done all, to stand. Stand therefore, having your loins girt about with truth, and having on the breastplate of righteousness; And your feet shod with the preparation of the gospel of peace; Above all, taking the shield of faith, wherewith ye shall be able to quench all the fiery darts of the wicked. And take the helmet of salvation, and the sword of the Spirit, which is the word of God: Praying always with all prayer and supplication in the Spirit, and watching thereunto with all perseverance and supplication for all saints; and for me, that utterance may be given unto me, that I may open my mouth boldly, to make known the mystery of the gospel, for which I am an ambassador in bonds: that therein I may speak boldly, as I ought to speak.

First, notice the connection Paul makes between prayer and boldness. He tells his partners to put on the whole armor of God and assume a position of attack through prayer. Then he tells them, "And while you're praying, pray that I might have boldness and utterance."

Notice that once again Paul is asking his partners, those in Ephesus, to pray for him to have boldness. And once again, he is acknowledging that the prayers of his partners have everything to do with his anointing to speak boldly the mystery of the gospel.

There is definitely a pattern. But the pattern doesn't end there.

As with his partners in Philippi, Paul not only asked his partners in Ephesus to pray, he expected them to pray. And by their prayers, he fully expected the Holy Spirit to supply him with all the boldness he needed. It was no different than his fully expecting to be supplied with all the finances and all the anointings he needed.

For Paul's boldness to be at the level he needed it to be to declare the mystery of the gospel in any situation, he needed his partners' prayers.

Granted, the actual boldness itself came from the Spirit of God, but it was all the prayers of agreement offered by Paul's partners that helped take this supernatural boldness to a higher level.

The bottom line was—Paul knew his partners' prayers were his success. ᴈ

No Spectators Here!

In all my years as a believer and as a minister of the gospel, I have observed how the Church has had a tendency to stand back and let the anointed ministers of God bear most of the weight of responsibility in carrying out the commandments of Jesus. Too often believers have sat back like an audience and watched as the pastors, evangelists, and so on did "the work."

That has never been God's intention. That is not His way.

Even when Jesus came to this earth to minister, He came needing help. He came looking for assistance. He came looking for assistants.

When Jesus came up from the waters of the Jordan River—having been baptized by John the Baptist—in that moment the Spirit of the Lord came upon Him and baptized Him for public ministry (John 1:29-34; Luke 4:18-19).

But while Jesus walked this earth bearing all the anointings of God, being the fullness of God manifested in the flesh,

He went up from those banks of the Jordan and chose 12 partners with whom to start His earthly ministry.

Have you ever noticed that each one of the 12 disciples—partners in ministry—was a businessman?

They were businessmen who knew nothing about ministry. Yet, Jesus needed partners and they were willing to leave the business world to serve Him.

But let's take that thought a step further.

Not only did Jesus need their partnership, but He also needed their prayers, just as we saw with the Apostle Paul's ministry.

In Matthew 26 and Mark 14, it is recorded that Jesus went to the garden in Gethsemane, along with His disciples—His partners—to pray.

In perhaps His greatest hour of need, Jesus looked to His partners for their support. He needed their presence and their prayers. And three different times during that spiritual night watch, He indicated that He needed their help.

As it turned out, that night watch in Gethsemane also happened to be one of the disciples' greatest hours of need, but they gave in to their flesh. They slept.

It is no different for you and me today.

We are in the middle of a night watch. We are watching...and waiting...for Jesus to return. And I'm sure you would agree that we as the Body of Christ are in our greatest hour of need.

If Jesus needed the prayers and support of His partners...if the Apostle Paul needed the prayers and support of his partners...Gloria and I certainly need the prayers and support of our Partners to complete what God has called us to do. All ministers of the gospel do.

If one of us can put a thousand to flight, and two of us can put 10,000 to flight (Deuteronomy 32:30)...imagine what more than a million KCM Partners can do—right now!

There isn't any tornado, or other weapon of destruction, safe on the face of this earth.

Study Questions

(1) What is one of the greatest "earthly" resources God has given us as believers? (Hint: It's the "heartbeat" of partnership.) _____

_____

_____

_____

(2) What two things did the Apostle Paul do in every prayer he prayed for his partners? (See Phlippians 1:3-5.) _____

_____

_____

(3) What one thing do Kenneth and Gloria Copeland do for their Partners each day? _____

_____

_____

(4) Explain the "prayer" dynamic of partnership involving you, Kenneth and Gloria Copeland, and other KCM Partners. _____

_____

_____

_____

(5) Explain the "subtle mind-set" we need to guard ourselves against when it comes to ministers of the gospel and the grace that is in/on their life and ministry. _____

_____

_____

_____

Study Questions

(6) What two things did the Apostle Paul draw on in order to receive the boldness he needed to do what he was called to do? (See Philippians 1:19-20.) _____

_____

_____

(7) Could it have been possible for Paul to fail in ministry? Explain.

_____

_____

(8) What two things did Paul specifically ask his partners to pray concerning his ministry? (See Ephesians 6:19-20.) _____

_____

_____

_____

(9) Did Jesus need partners in ministry? Who were His first partners? And what one thing did He ask/need them to do for Him? (See Matthew 26:36-44; Mark 14:26-39.) _____

_____

_____

(10) **Bonus question:** *If one KCM Partner can put 1,000 to flight, and two KCM Partners can put 10,000 to flight...how many can a million KCM Partners put to flight? (You do the math—and then believe with us for it!)* _____

_____

_____

Study Notes

"For I know that this shall turn to my
salvation through your prayer...."
Philippians 1:19

5

"Nevertheless to
abide in the flesh
[remain on this earth]
is more needful for
you. And having this
confidence, I know
that I shall abide
and continue with you
all for your furtherance
and joy of faith."

Philippians 1:24-25

CHAPTER FIVE
We're All About You

Partnership Requires a Willingness to Commit to Each Other

Our Commitment to You

A few years ago I was prompted by the Spirit of God to ask my Partners to send me a photograph—I wanted to see their faces.

Within weeks, we had tens of thousands of photographs. We were *covered* with smiling faces from all over the world. So we decided to start mounting them on special poster boards and displaying them around the ministry headquarters buildings in Fort Worth, Texas.

Today, it's quite a sight to walk through the halls and offices and *see* our Partners. It's a thrill for Gloria and me and our staff to see the people who stand alongside us in ministry, who support us with their faith, prayers, love and giving.

Now, what an honor and privilege it is for us to have *you* join these ranks of believers from around the world—and, yes, we want to add your photograph to our *family portrait* as soon as possible.

By now, you've probably figured out that I consider our partnership in ministry to be a very holy, sacred relationship established by God Almighty. It is a God-ordained relationship established on the principles of the Word— not man's ideas.

I guarantee that the relationship we now share in our covenant partnership is free from all *fleshly* pressures. It is free from any efforts or initiation on my part based on my "needs" or the "needs" of this ministry.

What I do, what Gloria does, what this ministry does...it's all about your needs. And it's about us—together—

It's about us— together— reaching a lost and dying world.

reaching a lost and dying world.

As I said earlier in this book, Gloria and I do what we do, say what we say and go where we go, all because of our Partners. We do it all because of you. You are always in our hearts.

My responsibility and commitment to you as my Partner is to pray for you and set my faith in agreement with you. You will never be without prayer again until Jesus comes. My commitment is to support you—and to seek God and find out how He wants me to minister to you. Those are all tremendous responsibilities.

It was that same sense of responsibility and commitment that caused Paul to wrestle with the idea of packing up and going on to heaven, or staying on this earth a while longer so he could meet the needs of his partners.

We find the reasoning behind his final decision in Philippians 1:21-25:

> For to me to live is Christ, and to die is gain. But if I live in the flesh, this is the fruit of my labour: yet what I shall choose I wot not. For I am in a strait betwixt two, having a desire to depart, and to be with Christ; which is far better: Nevertheless to abide in the flesh is more needful for you. And having this confidence, I know that I shall abide and continue with you all for your furtherance and joy of faith.

In the end, Paul decided to "abide and continue" with his partners. Heaven would have been gain, but there was still plenty of work that could be done for his partners. I believe Paul made that decision while he was actually writing his letter to them.

How do I know?

Because I have sensed that same kind of bonding and

draw in my own heart as I have written letters to my Partners.

Several years ago, the Lord cautioned me by saying, *Don't you dare write that [Partner] letter to get your needs met. You write that letter to get their needs met, and if you hold that letter up and you read it and you sense any part of it was written to get them to meet your needs, you throw it away and you start over.*

Over the years, writing the letter to my Partners each month has actually developed into an outlet of ministry like no other voice I have. It is my way of talking face to face with the thousands of men, women and children who are joined hand in hand with Gloria and me in our journey of faith.

Consequently, whatever personal challenges and victories I am in the middle of, my Covenant Partners know about them. Whatever God is telling me, my Partners are the first to know.

In fact, I estimate more than 95 percent of what I preach in our Believers' Conventions, Victory Campaigns and other meetings comes out of the revelation God gives me in my monthly ministry letter to my Partners.

Most of what I preach on television comes from praying over that Partner letter. I receive more revelation from God writing that letter than any other way.

So, I'm committed to seeking God and receiving revelation from Him that I can preach and teach to my Partners. Of course, other people are welcome to attend our meetings, watch our TV broadcast and listen to our teaching tapes and CDs. But I'm talking to my Partners 24/7. My heart is with them. ᶜᵉᴥ

Your Commitment to Us

Perhaps one of the most frequent questions new Partners ask is:

What does partnership with Kenneth Copeland Ministries require of me?

Partnership with any person or organization is based on relationship, much like we might think of a business partnership. In this case, however, our partnership is a covenant agreement centered on ministering the gospel to the world.

> *Partnership with any person or organization is based on relationship.*

So, like any relationship, partnership takes commitment on both parts. It requires a willingness to commit to each other.

In light of this, I simply ask that you pray and find out from God what *He* wants you to do where this ministry is concerned.

Does the Lord want you to pray for us every day? *(I believe so!)*

Does He want you to attend our meetings and maybe volunteer as an usher or counselor?

Does He want you to support us financially, or in some other way?

The point is, just begin by praying and seeking God's wisdom about it. He will show you what to do from there. And when He does—just do it.

6

"For this cause we also, since the day we heard it, do not cease to pray for you, and to desire that ye might be filled with the knowledge of his will in all wisdom and spiritual understanding."

Colossians 1:9

CHAPTER SIX
Dear Partner

*D*ear Partner,

Each month, when you receive your Partner letter from me, you will always find a list of handwritten scriptures at the close of the letter.

My Prayer for You

Father, I praise You and bless You and thank You
for my Partners. Lord, every prayer that's ever been prayed
for Gloria and me and all of us at Kenneth Copeland Ministries,
I thank You for it. I release my faith for them and with them
in every area of their lives.

Father, I pray the power of God—the Anointing of God—
that is in and on Gloria and me and the corporate anointing
that is in and on KCM be in the household and the ministry
and business affairs of every Partner we have. Let this anointing be on them as they minister and as they pray. Let it be on
them in the lives of their children to remove burdens and
destroy yokes, in the Name of Jesus.

Father, there are so many of them, I could not individ-
ually call each Partner's name before the throne of grace. I
would if I could. So I'm asking You by the Holy Spirit to
enter each Partner's name into these scriptures that I have
committed to pray over them every day of my life.

I'm asking You to enter their names into Psalm 23. Lord,
You are their Shepherd. They shall not want. You make them
lie down by the prospering green fields and lead them beside
the still waters.

I believe You for Your peace to rule in their lives. Even
though they may walk through the valley of the shadow of
death, they will fear no evil because You are with them. You
have prepared a table before them in the presence of their
enemies. You walk with them everywhere they go.

Father, I pray Psalm 91 and I say of the Lord, You are
their refuge and their fortress. You're their God and in You
they do trust.

Father, I pray Psalm 103 and all of its benefits for my
Partners. I thank You that their iniquities are forgiven—they

are completely wiped out. Thank You that sickness and disease are taken from their midst, and their youth is renewed like the eagle's. And I thank You that the angels of God take up their righteous cause. Hallelujah!

Father, I pray Isaiah 54:8-17 for all of my Partners. Great shall be the peace of their children; in righteousness they shall be established. They shall be far from oppression, for they shall not fear. They shall be far from terror, for it shall not come near them. Thank You, Lord, that no weapon formed against them can prosper.

Father, I pray Ephesians 1:16-23 for them. I thank You that the eyes of their understanding are opened, flooding their spirit with light of the power of the living God. Reveal to them what is the power toward us who believe, which You wrought when You raised Jesus from the dead. And, setting all things under His feet, gave Him to be the head over us who are His Body. We are the Body of the Anointed One. We are the Body of His Anointing. Hallelujah!

Father, I pray Ephesians 3:14-20, thanking You for a revelation that they are strengthened with might by Your Spirit in their spirit, that they comprehend with all the saints what is the length, the breadth, the height, and the depth and they know the love of the Anointed One. I thank You that they overflow with the anointing to love, and they know and are filled with the fullness of You who are able to do exceeding abundantly above all that we ask or think.

And, I pray Colossians 1:9-13, thanking You for delivering them from the authority of darkness and translating them into the kingdom of Your dear Son, strengthening them with might by Your Spirit in their spirit so that they walk worthy of You.

Finally, Lord, according to 1 Thessalonians 5:23, I thank You that You set apart my Partners wholly unto

Yourself—spirit, soul and body. They are preserved blameless unto the coming of our Lord Jesus, the Anointed One.

Now, Satan, I bind you and cast you out of all the affairs of my Partners.

I plead the blood of Jesus over every person, family, household, business, ministry and church that's in partnership with Kenneth Copeland Ministries. God, I praise You and thank You for it. I thank You for my Partners, Lord. Hallelujah! Bless the Lord, O my soul, and forget not all His benefits. Praise You, Jesus.

Now Lord, they have invested their goods, time, effort and prayer into this ministry.

Father, I'm asking You for supernatural harvest to come into their hands—the supernatural harvest of the former and the latter rain coming all at one time, such a harvest that the reapers catch up with the sowers.

I thank You for such a harvest that the moment it's sown, harvest time will be there, and they will reap it and bring it in. Exceeding abundantly beyond all that they even dare ask or think will flow into their lives—great, overflowing abundance of goods, resources, deliverance, healing, miracles—whatever it takes. Sweep their families into the kingdom. Give them the greatest ideas that have ever been born into the earth. Create whole industries from the ideas that You give my Partners.

I thank You for it, Lord. I give You the praise and the glory and the honor for it in the Name of Jesus. I declare with my faith, this year will be the grandest year in human history. Great shall be the peace of the Body of Christ and great shall be the peace of Jerusalem. Not a man-made peace that men are running around all over the world with, but the peace of God that passes all understanding. Peace that rules in the hearts of men—not just in their capital cities, politicians and politics. We'll not have politics as usual this year. I release my faith.

Now, Lord, I make demand on the promises. You said You would not have us to be ignorant of these end times—that You would not have us be ignorant of Your Word and Your affairs, You would not have us ignorant of the anointings, You would not have us ignorant of the seasons and the times we live in. I ask You for great revelation. I rebuke spiritual ignorance among us. I rebuke spiritual ignorance from among my Partners. Oh God, I receive the light from heaven—revelation of You, hallelujah!

For every apostle, prophet, evangelist, pastor, teacher, Sunday school teacher and minister of helps who is a Partner with this ministry, I receive revelation. Fill their pulpits with fire from heaven. And I give You the praise and the honor and the glory for it. Glory to God forevermore. I praise You for it, in Jesus' Name.

Amen.

Study Assignment

Write out and memorize the following scriptures. Then use them as a foundation for your prayers for yourself, your family, your friends and Kenneth Copeland Ministries:

(1) Psalm 23

(2) Psalm 91

(3) Psalm 103

(4) Isaiah 54

(5) Ephesians 1:16-23

(6) Ephesians 3:14-20

(7) Colossians 1:9-11

(8) 1 Thessalonians 5:23

Study Questions

(1) Psalm 23 _____

_____

_____

_____

_____

_____

_____

_____

_____

_____

_____

_____

_____

_____

_____

_____

_____

_____

_____

_____

_____

_____

_____

_____

_____

_____

_____

Study Questions

(2) Psalm 91 _____

_____

_____

_____

_____

_____

_____

_____

_____

_____

_____

_____

_____

_____

_____

_____

_____

_____

_____

_____

_____

_____

_____

_____

_____

_____

Study Questions

(3) Psalm 103 _____

_____

_____

_____

_____

_____

_____

_____

_____

_____

_____

_____

_____

_____

_____

_____

_____

_____

_____

_____

_____

_____

_____

_____

_____

Study Questions

(4) Isaiah 54 _____

_____

_____

_____

_____

_____

_____

_____

_____

_____

_____

_____

_____

_____

_____

_____

_____

_____

_____

_____

_____

_____

_____

_____

_____

Study Questions

(5) Ephesians 1:16-23 _____

_____

_____

_____

_____

_____

_____

_____

_____

_____

_____

(6) Ephesians 3:14-20 _____

_____

_____

_____

_____

_____

_____

_____

_____

_____

_____

Study Questions

(7) Colossians 1:9-11 _____

_____

_____

_____

_____

_____

_____

_____

_____

_____

_____

(8) 1 Thessalonians 5:23 _____

_____

_____

_____

_____

_____

_____

_____

_____

_____

_____

Mission Statement

The mission of Kenneth Copeland Ministries and Eagle Mountain International Church is to teach Christians worldwide who they are in Christ Jesus and how to live a victorious life in their covenant rights and privileges. The fulfillment of that mission takes place when those believers become rooted and grounded enough in God's Word to reach out and teach others these same principles.

- We are called to lead people, primarily born-again believers, to the place where they operate proficiently in the biblical principles of faith, love, healing, prosperity, redemption and righteousness, and to the place where they can share those principles with others.
- We are called to assist believers in becoming rooted, grounded and established in the Word of God by teaching them to give God's Word first place in their lives (Colossians 1:23; Psalm 112).
- We are called to reveal the mysteries, the victorious revelations of God's Word, that have been hidden from the ages (Colossians 1:25-28).
- We are called to build an army of mature believers, bringing them from milk to meat, from religion to reality. We are called to train them to become skillful in the word of righteousness, to stand firm in the spiritual warfare against the kingdom of darkness (Hebrews 5:12-14; Ephesians 6:10-18).
- We are called to proclaim that "Jesus Is Lord" from the top of the world to the bottom and all the way around.

This vision is being accomplished through the ministry efforts of Kenneth Copeland Ministries, Eagle Mountain International Church and staff on a worldwide scale through the local church and the use of television, campaigns, conventions, books, tapes, recordings and personal correspondence and is multiplied through the financial support of other ministries of like purpose.

Prayer for Salvation and Baptism in the Holy Spirit

Heavenly Father, I come to You in the Name of Jesus. Your Word says, "Whosoever shall call on the name of the Lord shall be saved" (Acts 2:21). I am calling on You. I pray and ask Jesus to come into my heart and be Lord over my life according to Romans 10:9-10. "If thou shalt confess with thy mouth the Lord Jesus, and shalt believe in thine heart that God hath raised him from the dead, thou shalt be saved. For with the heart man believeth unto righteousness; and with the mouth confession is made unto salvation." I do that now. I confess that Jesus is Lord, and I believe in my heart that God raised Him from the dead.

I am now reborn! I am a Christian—a child of Almighty God! I am saved! You also said in Your Word, "If ye then, being evil, know how to give good gifts unto your children: HOW MUCH MORE shall your heavenly Father give the Holy Spirit to them that ask him?" (Luke 11:13). I'm also asking You to fill me with the Holy Spirit. Holy Spirit, rise up within me as I praise God. I fully expect to speak with other tongues as You give me the utterance (Acts 2:4). In Jesus' Name. Amen!

Begin to praise God for filling you with the Holy Spirit. Speak those words and syllables you receive—not in your own language, but the language given to you by the Holy Spirit. You have to use your own voice. God will not force you to speak. Don't be concerned with how it sounds. It is a heavenly language!

Continue with the blessing God has given you and pray in the spirit every day.

You are a born-again, Spirit-filled believer. You'll never be the same!

Find a good church that boldly preaches God's Word and obeys it. Become a part of a church family who will love and care for you as you love and care for them.

We need to be connected to each other. It increases our strength in God. It's God's plan for us.

Make it a habit to watch the *Believer's Voice of Victory* television broadcast and become a doer of the Word, who is blessed in his doing (James 1:22-25).

About the Author

Kenneth Copeland is co-founder and president of Kenneth Copeland Ministries in Fort Worth, Texas, and best-selling author of books that include *Managing God's Mutual Funds—Yours and His, How to Discipline Your Flesh* and *Honor—Walking in Honesty, Truth and Integrity.*

Now in his 35th year as a minister of the gospel of Christ and teacher of God's Word, Kenneth is the recording artist of such award-winning albums as his Grammy nominated *Only the Redeemed, In His Presence, He Is Jehovah* and his most recently released *Just a Closer Walk.* He also co-stars as the character Wichita Slim in the children's adventure videos *The Gunslinger, Covenant Rider* and the movie *The Treasure of Eagle Mountain,* and as Daniel Lyon in the *Commander Kellie and the Superkids*_{SM} videos *Armor of Light* and *Judgment: The Trial of Commander Kellie.*

With the help of offices and staff in the United States, Canada, England, Australia, South Africa and Ukraine, Kenneth is fulfilling his vision to boldly preach the uncompromised Word of God from the top of this world, to the bottom, and all the way around. His ministry reaches millions of people worldwide through daily and Sunday TV broadcasts, magazines, teaching tapes and videos, conventions and campaigns, and the World Wide Web.

Learn more about
Kenneth Copeland Ministries
by visiting our Web site at
www.kcm.org

Books Available From
Kenneth Copeland Ministries

by Kenneth Copeland

*   A Ceremony of Marriage
    A Matter of Choice
    Covenant of Blood
    Faith and Patience—The Power Twins
*   Freedom From Fear
    Giving and Receiving
    Honor—Walking in Honesty, Truth and Integrity
    How to Conquer Strife
    How to Discipline Your Flesh
    How to Receive Communion
    In Love There Is No Fear
    Know Your Enemy
    Living at the End of Time—A Time of
          Supernatural Increase
    Love Never Fails
    Managing God's Mutual Funds—Yours and His
    Mercy—The Divine Rescue of the Human Race
*   Now Are We in Christ Jesus
    One Nation Under God (gift book with CD enclosed)
*   Our Covenant With God
    Partnership, Sharing the Vision—Sharing the Grace
*   Prayer—Your Foundation for Success
*   Prosperity: The Choice Is Yours
    Rumors of War
*   Sensitivity of Heart
*   Six Steps to Excellence in Ministry
*   Sorrow Not! Winning Over Grief and Sorrow
*   The Decision Is Yours
*   The Force of Faith
*   The Force of Righteousness
    The Image of God in You
    The Laws of Prosperity
*   The Mercy of God (Available in Spanish only)
    The Outpouring of the Spirit—The Result of Prayer
*   The Power of the Tongue
    The Power to Be Forever Free
*   The Winning Attitude

*Available in Spanish

Turn Your Hurts Into Harvests
Walking in the Realm of the Miraculous
* Welcome to the Family
* You Are Healed!
Your Right-Standing With God

by Gloria Copeland

* And Jesus Healed Them All
Are You Listening?
Are You Ready?
Be a Vessel of Honor
Build Your Financial Foundation
Fight On!
Go With the Flow
God's Prescription for Divine Health
God's Success Formula
God's Will for You
God's Will for Your Healing
God's Will Is Prosperity
* God's Will Is the Holy Spirit
* Harvest of Health
Hidden Treasures
Living Contact
Living in Heaven's Blessings Now
* Love—The Secret to Your Success
No Deposit—No Return
Pleasing the Father
Pressing In—It's Worth It All
Shine On!
The Grace That Makes Us Holy
The Power to Live a New Life
The Protection of Angels
The Secret Place of God's Protection (gift book with CD enclosed)
The Unbeatable Spirit of Faith
* Walk in the Spirit (Available in Spanish only)
Walk With God
Well Worth the Wait
Words That Heal (gift book with CD enclosed)
Your Promise of Protection—The Power of
    the 91st Psalm

Books Co-Authored by
Kenneth and Gloria Copeland

Family Promises
Healing Promises
Prosperity Promises
Protection Promises

* From Faith to Faith—A Daily Guide to Victory
From Faith to Faith—A Perpetual Calendar

One Word From God Series
• One Word From God Can Change Your Destiny
• One Word From God Can Change Your Family
• One Word From God Can Change Your Finances
• One Word From God Can Change Your Formula
  for Success
• One Word From God Can Change Your Health
• One Word From God Can Change Your Nation
• One Word From God Can Change Your
  Prayer Life
• One Word From God Can Change Your
  Relationships

Over The Edge—A Youth Devotional
Load Up—A Youth Devotional
Pursuit of His Presence—A Daily Devotional
Pursuit of His Presence—A Perpetual Calendar

Other Books Published by KCP

The First 30 Years—A Journey of Faith
    The story of the lives of Kenneth and
        Gloria Copeland.
Real People. Real Needs. Real Victories.
    A book of testimonies to encourage your faith.

John G. Lake—His Life, His Sermons, His
    Boldness of Faith

*Available in Spanish

The Holiest of All by Andrew Murray
The New Testament in Modern Speech
   by Richard Francis Weymouth
Unchained by Mac Gober

Products Designed for Today's Children and Youth

And Jesus Healed Them All (confession book and CD gift package)
Baby Praise Board Book
Baby Praise Christmas Board Book
Noah's Ark Coloring Book
The Best of *Shout!* Adventure Comics
The *Shout!* Giant Flip Coloring Book
The *Shout!* Joke Book
The *Shout!* Super-Activity Book
Wichita Slim's Campfire Stories

***Commander Kellie and the Superkids*_{SM} Books:**
The SWORD Adventure Book
*Commander Kellie and the Superkids*_{SM}
Solve-It-Yourself Mysteries
*Commander Kellie and the Superkids*_{SM}
Adventure Series: Middle Grade Novels by
Christopher P.N. Maselli

> #1 The Mysterious Presence
> #2 The Quest for the Second Half
> #3 Escape From Jungle Island
> #4 In Pursuit of the Enemy
> #5 Caged Rivalry
> #6 Mystery of the Missing Junk
> #7 Out of Breath
> #8 The Year Mashela Stole Christmas

World Offices
of Kenneth Copeland Ministries

For more information about KCM and a free
catalog, please write the office nearest you:

Kenneth Copeland Ministries
Fort Worth, Texas 76192-0001

Kenneth Copeland
Locked Bag 2600
Mansfield Delivery Centre
QUEENSLAND 4122
AUSTRALIA

Kenneth Copeland
Post Office Box 15
BATH
BA1 3XN
U.K.

Kenneth Copeland
Private Bag X 909
FONTAINEBLEAU
2032
REPUBLIC OF SOUTH AFRICA

Kenneth Copeland
Post Office Box 378
Surrey, B.C.
V3T 5B6
CANADA

Kenneth Copeland Ministries
Post Office Box 84
L'VIV 79000
UKRAINE

We're Here for You!

Believer's Voice of Victory Television Broadcast

Join Kenneth and Gloria Copeland and the *Believer's Voice of Victory* broadcasts Monday through Friday and on Sunday each week, and learn how faith in God's Word can take your life from ordinary to extraordinary. This teaching from God's Word is designed to get you where you want to be—*on top!*

You can catch the *Believer's Voice of Victory* broadcast on your local, cable or satellite channels.

*Check your local listings for times and stations in your area.

Believer's Voice of Victory Magazine

Enjoy inspired teaching and encouragement from Kenneth and Gloria Copeland and guest ministers each month in the *Believer's Voice of Victory* magazine. Also included are real-life testimonies of God's miraculous power and divine intervention in the lives of people just like you!

It's more than just a magazine—it's a ministry.

Shout! The Voice of Victory for Kids

Shout!...The dynamic magazine just for kids is a Bible-charged, action-packed, bimonthly magazine available FREE to kids everywhere! Featuring Wichita Slim and *Commander Kellie and the Superkids*_{SM}, *Shout!* is filled with colorful adventure comics, challenging games and puzzles, exciting short stories, solve-it-yourself mysteries and much more!!

Stand up, sign up and get ready to *Shout!*

To receive a FREE subscription to
Believer's Voice of Victory, or to give a child you
know a FREE subscription to *Shout!*, write to:

Kenneth Copeland Ministries
Fort Worth, Texas 76192-0001
Or call:
1-800-600-7395
(7 a.m.-5 p.m. CT)
Or visit our Web site at:
www.kcm.org

If you are writing from outside the U.S., please contact the KCM office nearest you. Addresses for all Kenneth Copeland Ministries offices are listed on the previous page.

KENNETH COPELAND MINISTRIES